LITTLE LEARNERS
On the Farm

KATHRYN SELBERT
LISA REGAN

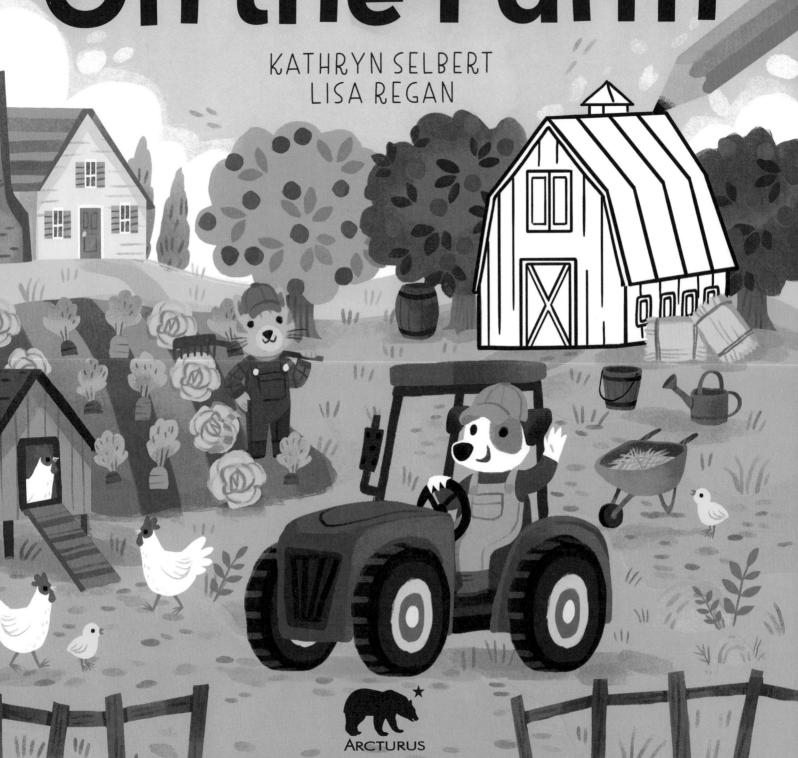

ARCTURUS

ARCTURUS

This edition published in 2024 by Arcturus Publishing Limited
26/27 Bickels Yard, 151–153 Bermondsey Street,
London SE1 3HA

Author: Lisa Regan
Illustrator: Kathryn Selbert
Editor: Lydia Halliday
Designer: Nathan Balsom
Managing Editor: Joe Harris
Design Manager: Rosie Bellwood-Moyler

ISBN: 978-1-3988-4362-2
CH011565NT
Supplier 29, Date 0624, PI 00007366

Printed in China

There is so much to see and do on a farm! People are always busy, with animals to look after or fields to take care of. Test yourself with these fun puzzles—count the crops, find foods as they grow, and work your way through all kinds of farm-themed mazes. All you need is a pen or pencil, and some crayons.

What are you waiting for? Let's get puzzling!

Let's go!

Farmer Mo loves to drive his tractor from field to field. Which of the shadow shapes matches Farmer Mo's tractor?

Ripe and ready

These juicy apples look delicious!
Are there more apples on the
trees, or on the ground?

Have you any wool?

Can you spot the five differences between these two groups of sheep?

Baby boom!

This mother pig has eight piglets. The biggest has
a number 1 on it, and the smallest has a number 8.
Number the other pigs 2 to 7, in order of their size.

Fresh and delicious

It's time for strawberry picking! Which of the puzzle pieces fits exactly back into the picture?

A   B   C

Home sweet home

The farm cat is taking time off! See if you can find eight things that are different in the second picture.

In the meadow

Lots of wild animals make their homes on farmland. Can you find each of these rabbits, plus an extra one in the field?

A B C D E

A strong scent

Onions grow in the ground, and you can often smell them! Find a way through this onion patch from start to finish.

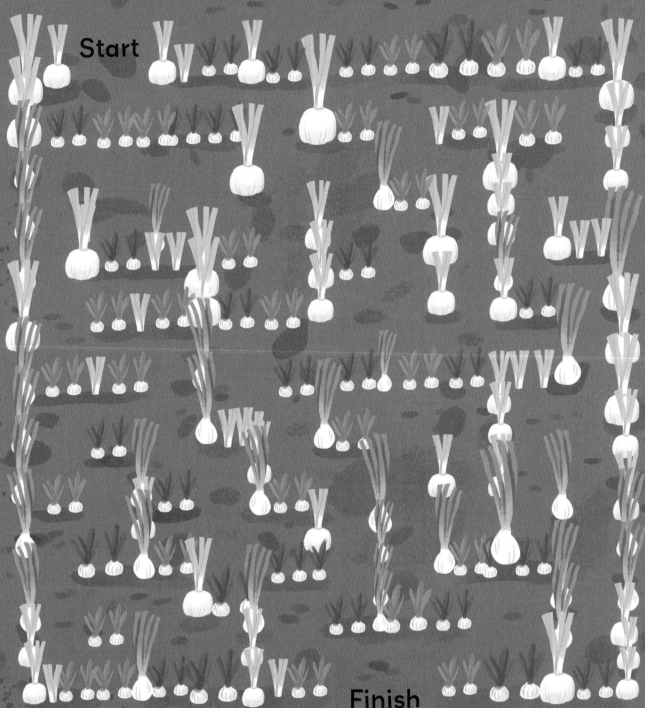

Start

Finish

Busy bees

Bees help farmers in lots of ways. We love bees!
Find the four bees that are going back to the hive.

Donkey drawing

Learn how to draw a donkey by following the simple steps.

Greedy goats!

Which goat ate the flowers?
Use the clues to help you.

It is white and brown.

It has long, floppy ears.

Pumpkin patch

Finish this picture using your pens or crayons.

Stay away

Some bugs are not welcome on a farm! Fill in the grid so that each row, column, and grid of four has one of each bug in it.

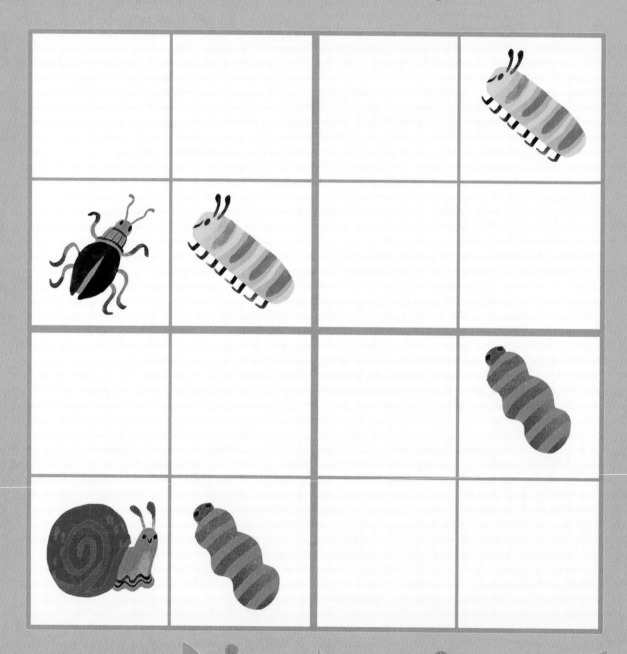

A job to do

Copy the picture of the scarecrow
so there is one in the empty space.

Round and round

A farmer uses lots of different machines to get the farm work done. How many wheels can you count in this picture?

Pecking order

Chickens love to eat greens and grains. Which four of these hens are exactly the same?

Daily bread

Some farmers grow wheat, and sell it so bakers can make bread. Match these different types of bread into pairs and find one on its own.

Five a day

Vegetables are so good for you! You should try to eat lots of them. How many are there of each?

Bird watching

You might spot this big bird in farmland or woodland. It is a pheasant. Can you also spot four things that have moved in the second picture?

Crunchy and tasty

Some vegetables taste wonderful in a salad. See if you can find each of the items below in the main picture.

Coffee to go

Coffee is grown on farms. Which path takes the tractor past the highest number of baskets of coffee beans?

Pond life

Which of the daddy ducks is the odd one out?
And how many ducklings can you count?

A simple sheep

Sheep are happiest when they are together in a flock. Copy this sheep so the field is full of them.

Rice is nice

Rice needs lots of water to grow properly.
Which of the small squares is not in the big picture?

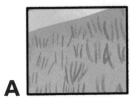
A

B

C

D

Hello horse!

This horse looks a bit lost. Join the dots, from 1 to 20, to finish the picture.

Sunny days?

Sunflowers are grown for their seeds. Birds love them! Look carefully at this picture and see how many bees and butterflies you can count.

Harvest time

When the crops are ripe, it's time to harvest them. Help this farmer through the field of wheat to get to his harvester.

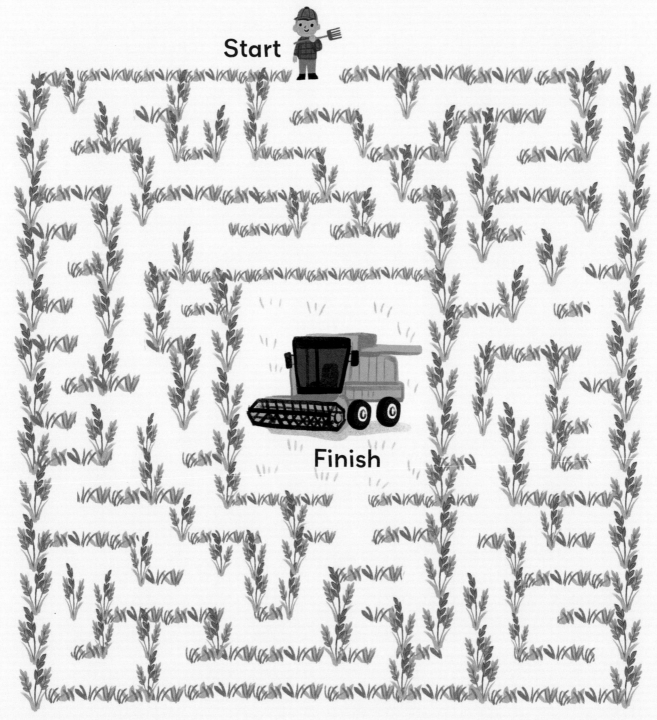

Start

Finish

Fruit picking

The fruit is ready to harvest.
Follow the lines to see who picks each fruit.

A beautiful sight

Butterflies visit flowers to drink their sweet nectar, and carry pollen as they go. How many blue butterflies can you see? And how many red ones?

Hard at work

These farmers have a lot to do. See if you can fit each of the pieces below back into the puzzle.

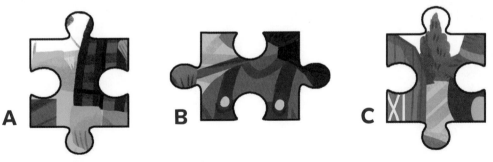

A   B   C

Feeding time

These pigs are hungry! See if you can find eight things that are different in the second picture.

Small things

Some insects and bugs are a farmer's friend, but not all of them. See if you can find each of the minibeasts below on the edge of the farmland.

Your turn!

Can you help to finish this picture
with your pens and crayons?

Birds of a feather

Birds are some of the noisiest members of a farm! Which of the small squares is not seen in the big picture?

A

B

C

D

E

Vine time

Grapes are grown on farms called vineyards.
Cross out all the letters G and M to find four
countries famous for their vineyards.

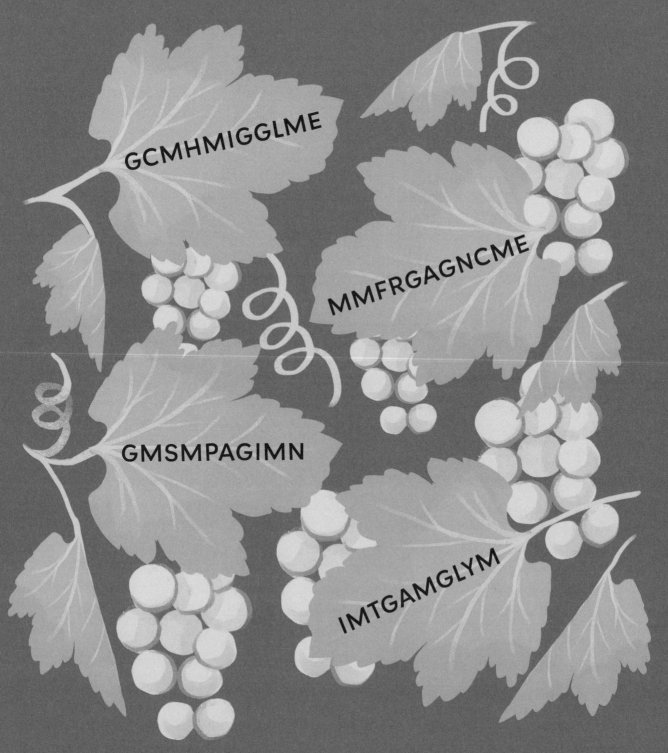

GCMHHMIGGLME

MMFRGAGNCME

GMSMPAGIMN

IMTGAMGLYM

In the orchard

Pears grow on trees in an orchard. See how many pears you can count in this picture.

Horsing around

Horses are useful for transport, especially where there are no roads. Which of the shadow shapes matches this beautiful horse?

Something delicious

What has Farmer Green grown?
Join the dots to find out.

Proud as a peacock

Farmer Flo keeps peacocks in her yard. Finish the one below to make it as beautiful as the others.

Time for tea

Many of the fresh foods you eat come from farm products. Find a way through the maze to get from handwashing to the table. Yummy!

Start

Finish

Lucy Goosey

Lucy Goosey is the biggest goose on the farm. Put the others in order, with number 1 for the biggest and number 6 for the smallest.

Lucy
Goosey

Amazing maize

It's tasty AND it's good for you! See if you can find eight things that are different in the second picture.

Four of a kind

Which four of Farmer Lola's cows are exactly the same?

Starting the day

Lots of breakfast items are made from cereal crops. Find out what each farmer has for breakfast by following the lines.

Market day

Farmer Chuck has a stall at the market. Fill in the squares by counting the different foods you see.

Lovely llamas

Llamas can be kept on a farm, too! Use the clues to work out which is the naughtiest llama here.

It doesn't have white wool.

There are no spots on its head or body.

Many mice

These little mice are hoping to grab some grains of wheat. Which mouse looks slightly different to all the others?

Fruit farm

Apples grow on trees. Find the puzzle piece that finishes this picture.

Your turn

Learn how to draw a tractor by
following these simple steps.

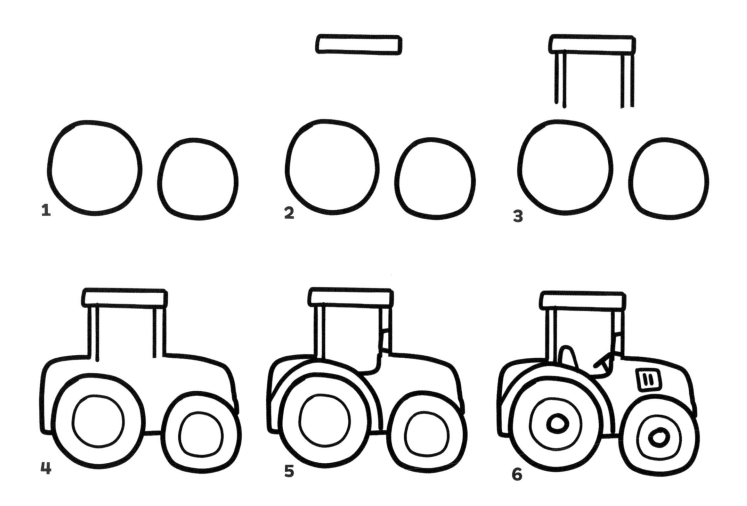

Something's missing

Fill in the missing letters to spell the weather you see in each picture.

S_N

RAI_

_NOW

__ORM

Cuddly sheep

See if you can find eight things that are different in the second picture.

Flowery fun

Farmer Flo is making her yard look pretty. Which flower should she plant next to continue the pattern?

In the fields

It is harvest time. Finish the
picture using your pens and crayons.

Made of wheat

Wheat can be made into lots of different foods.
Fill in the grid so that each row, column, and
grid of four, has one of each food in it.

Quack quack!

Look carefully at the big picture.
Can you find each of the creatures below?

From the ground

What has Farmer Gru picked for his dinner?
Join the different sets of dots to find out.

Run around

Ossie the ostrich lives on a farm. Help her find the path with numbers that add up to the highest total.

From tiny seeds

Cross out the letters that appear twice.
The remaining letters will spell the names
of the vegetables in the seed packets.

HCHORSNSGG

FBFEAPPNDSD

TUERNMEIPMS

Feathered friends

Which five of these chicks are exactly the same as each other?

Half and half

Copy the other half of the picture into the blank space to finish the drawing of the pig.

Going bananas

Bananas can be grown on farms in hot countries. Find a way through the banana maze from start to finish, without crossing any banana skins.

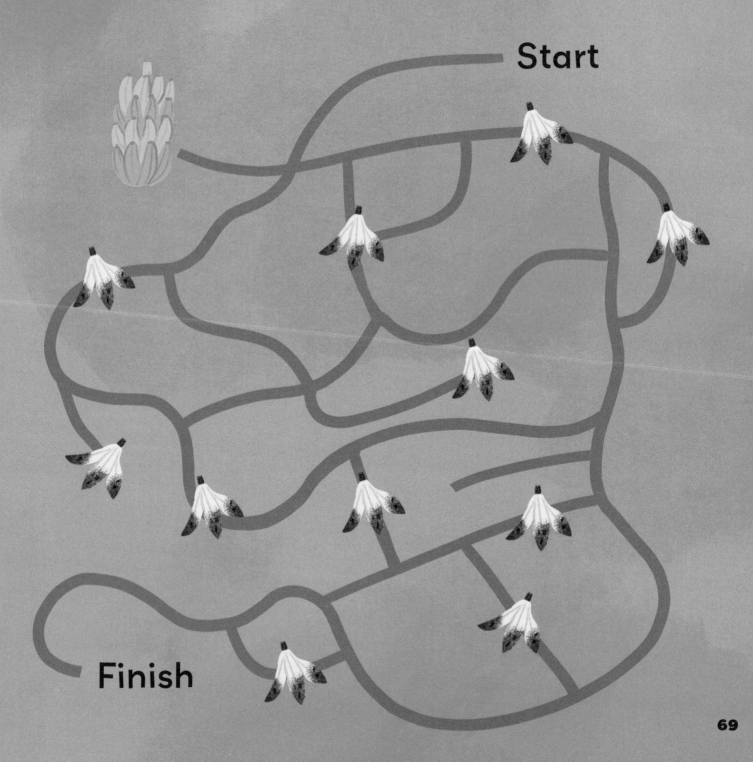

Start

Finish

Busy bees

These bees are very busy indeed! See if you can find eight things that are different in the second picture.

A tasty treat

Chocolate is made from cocoa beans, which grow on trees. Can you find three beautiful birds in these trees?

Where's the rabbit?

Can you spot the rabbits in this field? See if you can fit each of the pieces back into the puzzle.

A

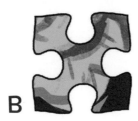
B

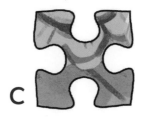
C

Going for a ride

Using the patterns to help you, match each horse with a rider.

Tulip fields

This is one of the most beautiful farms you'll see! Finish the rest of the picture with your pens and crayons.

Making hay

This field has been harvested and the hay bundled into bales. Which three things have moved in the bottom picture?

Let's try!

Learn how to draw a goose
by following these simple steps.

Look at me!

Which of the shadow shapes
matches the scarecrow?

All terrain vehicles

Which of the ATVs belongs to Farmer Midge?
Use the clues to work it out.

It isn't red.

It has yellow wheels.

The end of the day

Farmer Pete is heading for home! See if you can find eight things that are different in the second picture.

In the stables

These horses are waiting to be fed. See if you can find each of the items below in the main picture.

Lovely lemons

Shh! Farmer Fred is having a nap by his lemon tree. How many lemons can you count?

Beautiful butterflies

Which of the butterflies is slightly different from the others?

Answers

Page 4

The answer is E.

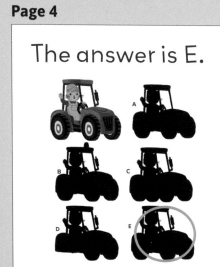

Page 5

There are more apples on the trees (15) than on the ground (12).

Pages 6-7

Page 8

Page 9

Pages 10-11

Page 12

The rabbit in the red circle is the extra one.

Page 13

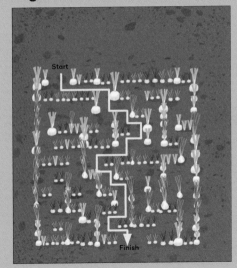

Page 14

Page 16

Page 18

Page 20

There are 10 wheels.

Page 21

Page 22

Page 23

Page 24

Page 25

Page 26

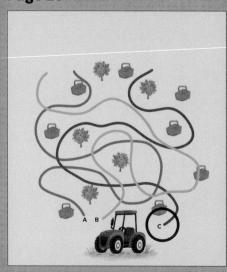

Page 27

There are 8 ducklings.

Page 29

Page 30

Page 31

There are 4 butterflies and 6 bees.

Page 32

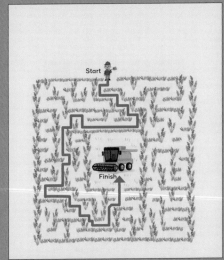

Page 33

Page 34

There are 8 blue butterflies and 10 red ones.

Page 35

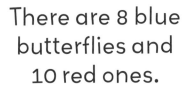

Pages 36-37

Page 38

Page 40

Page 41

The answers are:
CHILE
FRANCE
SPAIN
ITALY

Page 42

There are
24 pears.

Page 43

The answer is D.

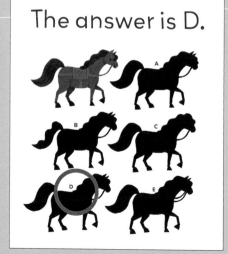

Page 44

Page 46

Page 47

Pages 48-49

Page 50

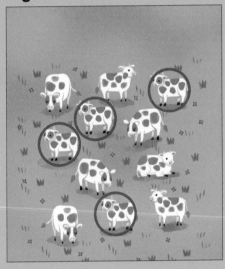

Page 51

Page 52

91

Page 53

Page 54

Page 55

Page 57

SUN RAIN

SNOW STORM

Pages 58-59

Page 60

Add a white flower.

Page 62

Page 63

Page 64

Page 65

The answer is C.

Page 66

Answers:
CORN
BEANS
TURNIPS

Page 67

Page 69

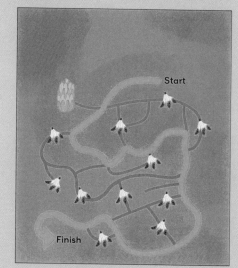

Pages 70-71

Page 72

94

Page 73

Page 74

Page 76

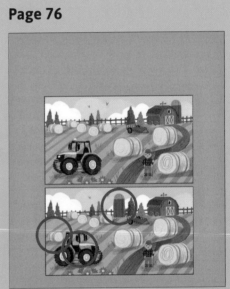

Page 78

Page 79

Pages 80-81

Page 82

Page 83

There are 20 lemons.

Page 84

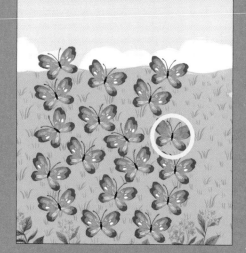